Giuseppino De Roma

Francis of Assisi

ST PAULS

FRANCIS OF ASSISI
Original title: *Francesco d'Assisi*
© 1992 Figlie di San Paolo, Milan, Italy

English edition
© 1995, ST PAULS, Homebush, Australia

Translation by Marie Therese Levey RSJ

Australian edition:
First published, October 1995
National Library of Australia
Card and ISBN number 1 875570 64 0

Illustrations: Carla Ruffinelli

Published by
ST PAULS — Society of St Paul
60-70 Broughton Road — (PO Box 230) — Homebush NSW 2140

ST PAULS is an activity of the Priests and Brothers of the Society of St Paul who proclaim the Gospel through the media of social communication.

Francis chooses to be poor

Francis was born in Assisi in the winter of 1181. His father, who was a business man, was Peter Bernardone, and his mother's name was Pica. His father, a stern man who was used to being in charge, wanted his son to become a rich trader. When young Francis asked if he could become a knight, Peter spared no expense in the cost. He prepared for him a splendid suit of armour and bought him a very beautiful horse.

Francis got ready to leave for war, but on the day before going he heard a voice which said to him:

'Why do you want to become a knight in the service of a count? Why not instead join the service of a prince?'

Francis understood that the prince was Jesus, and from that day he thought of entering the service of the Lord. But he did not know how to become a knight of Jesus.

One day, when he was twenty-five, Francis happened to pass by the little church of St Damian in the plain of Assisi.

The church was abandoned and was falling into ruins. Francis entered and knelt down in front of a large crucifix. And behold a voice, which seemed to come from the crucifix, spoke to him:

'Francis, my house is falling down. Fix it up.'

Francis understood by this that to be a knight of God meant giving oneself to the service of the poor in the church of the Lord. So he gave up his family home, left his father completely, even the clothes which he had on, and gave himself to repairing the little church of St Damian.

Francis was always happy since he had become a true knight. He had a very sweet, melodious voice. Often he sang songs of praise, glory and honour to the most high and almighty God.

With his companions Francis goes to the pope in Rome

Very soon other young men of Assisi joined Francis. Then he said to them:

'My brothers, I see that almighty and merciful God will continue to increase our community. Let us go then to Rome and let us ask the holy father's permission to continue our rule of life according to the gospel, as true knights of Christ.'

Francis' proposal pleased the brothers and the group set out towards Rome. They walked barefoot with cheerful hearts, singing the praises of the most high. Nature, which surrounded them, seemed to share their joy.

The sun shone high in the heavens, a symbol and image of God who lights up the mind and warms the hearts of all. Francis pointed this out to the brothers and said:

'Look brothers, the sun is the highest of all creatures. It shines during the day and give us light. Let us praise God through this our beautiful brother, radiant and full of splendour.'

The brothers reached Rome and were received by Pope Innocent III. Francis explained to the pope his proposal of living in obedience and chastity, and in possessing nothing of his own, according to the example of the blessed Lord Jesus. The pope approved the rule and authorised the friars to preach the holy gospel everywhere.

As well, a young girl of Assisi called Clare (a word which means 'light'), followed the example of Francis and joined him in the now-repaired monastery of St Damian. Here, Clare and other companions lived a hidden life in the observance of the most rigid poverty.

Clare and the moon in the well

One day blessed Francis travelled far from Assisi in company with Brother Leo, also named 'little lamb of God'. It was dusk and the sun was setting behind the lovely hills of Tuscany. The two brothers sat on a large stone near a farm shed. From the knapsack they took out a piece of dry and black bread, and after a blessing to the heavenly Father, they began to eat.

Then they found a place in the hayloft of a shed and Brother Leo soon fell asleep. Francis instead stayed awake a long time in prayer. He contemplated the star-filled sky. He gazed at the moon which, high in the heavens, lit up the night.

'I praise you, O my Lord, for all your creatures. I praise you for Sister Moon and the stars. You have formed them in the heavens, clear, precious and beautiful.'

So blessed Francis prayed while Brother Leo slept peacefully. Then Francis — the little poor man — approached a well that was near the hut.

He leaned over the edge of the well.

The moon, high in the heavens, was reflected in the water of the well. The water rippled lightly and the moon seemed to be a smiling human face. Suddenly Francis was taken by a great joy. He woke Brother Leo and said to him excitedly:

'O Brother Leo, little lamb of God! Look inside the well. Do you see the laughing face of Sister Clare in the moon's reflection? The most high God lets me see the face of Clare reflected in this deep and calm water; God wants me to understand that our Sister at St Damian smiles and is well.'

'And thus it is in truth,' responded Brother Leo, still half asleep.

Brother Wind and Sister Water

Blessed Francis loved all the creatures of the Lord, whether they had life or not. He praised and blessed God not only for the living creatures, like animals, plants and flowers, but also for the wind, the rain, the hail, the cold and the heat, the storm and the calm. All these creatures he called by the name of brothers and sisters.

One day Francis decided to embark on a ship. He wanted to go to Marocco to preach the gospel. But the ship was caught up by unfavourable winds and Francis was forced to disembark and, for the moment, to give up his project of preaching the gospel to the fierce Saracens.

'Brother Wind,' commented Francis to the brothers, 'does not want me to go elsewhere. The time to go to Marocco is not yet right. This is the will of the Lord. He has brought me Brother Wind today with his mighty voice.'

A particular favourite of Francis was Sister Water. The love of blessed Francis for Sister Water was so great that she obeyed him like an intelligent creature.

One summer day the man of God wanted to climb a high mountain in order to dedicate himself to solitude and prayer. Since he was weak and sick through long penances and fasting, he asked a local farmer to carry him to the top of the mountain on the back of his donkey.

The mountain was dry and rocky, with very hard stones. There was not a blade of grass, nor a brook nor a spring there. At a certain point the farmer, tired out by the long and difficult journey, and exhausted with the heat, began to complain:

'I am struck with thirst! If I do not find water soon I will die of thirst.'

Blessed Francis got off the donkey and knelt among the sharp stones. He prayed to the Lord, then said to the man:

'Go quickly behind that rock and you will find there a spring of very pure water.'

'One thing I know,' replied the man with the dry throat, 'that on this mountain there has never existed any spring. I know this place well.'

The little poor man responded:

'Our Sister Water obeys the command of the Lord. I have prayed to the most high and God has heard me. God has made the water spring from this hard stone.'

The farmer ran behind the rock and found to his amazement a fountain of fresh, clear water. The man drank well at that font and so did the donkey, since he was as thirsty as the master.

Brother Fire

Above all the creatures not endowed with life, Francis loved, with a special tenderness, Brother Fire. Often he said to the friars:

'My dear sons, when the night descends, each man should praise God for Brother Fire. By means of it, in fact, our eyes are lit up in the dark. We are all like blind men and through this brother the Lord gives light to our eyes.'

Francis suffered greatly when anyone failed to show respect for the fire. He considered the fire a creature almost sensible and gifted with intelligence.

One winter's day he sat in contemplation beside the fire. Suddenly a spark fell on his tunic without his noticing it. Very soon the tunic began to burn and blessed Francis noticed his leg was very hot. The brother who sat beside him, noticing the fire beginning, ran at once to take a jug of water to put out the fire. But blessed Francis said to him:

'My dear brother, I beg you not to hurt Brother Fire.'

And he would not allow in any way the fire to be extinguished. Then the brother dashed to the superior of the convent where Francis then resided. At once the superior came and ordered Francis, in virtue of holy obedience, to allow the fire to be extinguished. Only then Francis consented for the jug to be emptied onto the tunic.

It was holiness such as this that showed through this beautiful, happy, healthy and strong brother, who never wanted to extinguish the candle or the lamp; but always left these tasks to the right companions. For him, to extinguish the fire was like killing a brother.

Our Mother Earth

Beside the little church of St Mary of the Angels, where the blessed one lived, there was a piece of earth. The brother gardener cultivated plants and vegetables there for the brothers to eat.

Often Francis stood in the vegetable garden to think about the beauty of the plants, of the flowers and of each blade of grass. He said to the friars:

'Brothers, our mother earth gives many fruits in order to sustain our bodies, and coloured flowers so that we can praise the most high. Each creature, in fact, with its voice, its perfume, and its colours, says: ''God has created me for you, O people''.'

To the friar who cut the wood and prepared it for the fire, Francis recommended with a voice broken from weeping:

'O brother, do not hurt the tree cutting the still living branches. But break only the dry branches, so that this our brother does not have too much to suffer.'

To the friar who cultivated the garden he said frequently:

'Do not plant only eatable grasses, but plant also some flowers because with their perfume and their colours they glorify the Lord who has created them.'

When the man of God, walking through the streets, saw expanses of flowers, he stopped and invited them to praise the most high. And he did this with the crops, and the vines and the forests and the fields.

Above all blessed Francis showed his most tender love towards the animals. Each animal, from the wolf to the cricket, from the donkey to the skylark, he considered as his brother or sister.

He gathered from the earth insects or worms so that they would not be trampled on and, before returning them to the grass, looked tenderly at them on the palm of his hand. To the bees he wanted to administer some honey and the best wine, so that they would not suffer starvation in the rigour of the winter.

But amongst all the animals, he loved in particular those more tame, like the sheep, the lambs and the birds. And all these creatures on their part strived to reciprocate the love of the saint and to repay him with their gratitude.

They seemed happy and laughing when he stroked them, gave signs of assent when he questioned them, obeyed when he commanded.

The canticle of the creatures

By now the earthly life of Francis turned towards its close. In the autumn of 1224, at the age of forty-three, Francis went up onto the mountain of La Verna in Tuscany to give himself to prayer.

There he knelt on a high rock, prayed to the Lord Jesus crucified. And while he prayed he received on his hands, on his feet, and on his chest the same wounds as the crucifix.

Francis was brought into the monastery of St Damian. In the little garden of the monastery a hut was prepared so that the saint could rest. During one night, while the blessed one was tormented by great suffering, he received from the Lord the assurance of the eternal prize. Then Francis, taken by great joy, composed the Canticle of Brother Sun.

For two long years before his death, Francis carried on his body the wounds of the crucifix.

In the spring of 1226, the bishop of Assisi, knowing that Francis' health was deteriorating, commanded him to remain as a guest near him to receive necessary treatment.

While Francis found himself a patient near the bishop's palace, it happened that the bishop and the mayor of Assisi had a deep disagreement. Then Francis said to the friars:

'It is a great shame for our brothers that the bishop and the mayor are not in peace with each other. Perhaps we have not given them the right example. O Brother Leo, take then the pen and add this verse to the Canticle of Brother Sun:

'May you be praised, my Lord, through those who forgive out of love for you,
and through those who bear infirmity and tribulation.
Blessed are those who endure in peace,
Because they will be crowned by you.'

Then Francis called the mayor and the bishop to his bedside. He recited the following verses of the Canticle:

Most High, all powerful, good Lord,
To you be all praise, glory, honour and blessing.
To you alone, most high, they belong
And no one is worthy to mention your name.
May you be praised, O my Lord, with all your creatures,
Especially Brother Sun,
Who shines during the day and gives us light.
He is beautiful, radiant and full of splendour.
And is a symbol and image of you, most high.
May you be praised my Lord through Sister Moon and the stars:
You have formed them in the heavens clear, precious and beautiful.
May you be praised, O my Lord, through Brother Wind;
Through the sky — cloudy and serene — and each kind of weather
Through whom all your creatures are sustained.
May you be praised O my Lord, through Sister Water.
Who is very useful, humble, precious and chaste.
May you be praised, O my Lord, through Brother Fire,
Through whom you light up the night:
He is beautiful, cheerful, robust and strong.
May you be praised, my Lord, for our sister, Mother Earth,
Who sustains and governs us,
And produces various fruits with coloured flowers and grasses.

When blessed Francis recited with the brothers the verses of forgiveness, the bishop and the mayor of Assisi embraced as brothers, and were reconciled.

Sister Death

Towards the end of the month of September 1226, Brother Elias, who lovingly assisted in the service of God, said to Francis:

'Father, your life has been a torch and a model for the friars and for the entire Church of God. So also will be your death. Father, know then that there remains little of life, for so the doctors have predicted.'

Then Francis, although broken by illness and almost blind, radiant with a deep joy, responded in a thin voice:

'O Brother Elias, thanks for the good news that you have given me. If then my death is close, call Brother Angelo and Brother Leo.'

At once Elias called the two friars. When these were at the side of blessed Francis' bed, he said to Brother Leo:

'O little lamb of God, take notice and write the last verse which I want added now to the Canticle of Brother Sun.'

And, almost singing, the poor man said:

'Praised be to you, my Lord, through our Sister Bodily Death, From whom no living person can escape.
Blessed those whom Sister Death will find in your most holy will.
Praise and bless my Lord
Give thanks and serve him with great humility.'

Having finished this verse, Brother Francis said to Brother Angelo and to Brother Leo:

'And now, O brothers, the canticle is complete. Sing it all through and I, as much as I can, will sing it with you.'

With tears in their eyes and with trembling voices, the two companions followed the orders of their most beloved father, while blessed Francis, moving his lips, accompanied them with his weak voice.

And to that song was united, invisible but present, all the creatures that the poor man had loved so much. And united also were the voices of all the children of the world who loved so much the little poor man of Assisi.

The last will of Francis

On the evening of October 3, feeling by now that death was very close, Francis was placed on the bare earth right beside the little church of St Mary of the Angels where he had begun his work of perfection.

Then he called around him all the brothers who lived in that place. At his left stood Brother Elias, Vicar of the Order, and around in a circle were Brother Bernard, Brother Egidio, Brother Phillip, Brother Masseo, Brother Leo, little lamb of God, and many others.

Francis held his hands crossed on his chest and, after having blessed the city of Assisi, turned back to his friars and said:

'Goodbye, all my sons. Live in the love of God. Love all God's creatures. As for me, I must hurry to meet the Lord. I am confident of reaching God whom I have loved and served as would a true knight.'

Francis extended his arms then in the form of a cross and said:

'I, though a poor and little man, can bless you in the name of the most high.'

Then he made them carry the book of the gospel and read a passage. When the reading was finished, the man of God began to recite a psalm and said:

'With my voice I cry out to the Lord.'

And he recited it to the last verse:

'Remember the good I have done, O Lord, at the moment in which you give me the reward.'

Then, knowing that he would become dust, he asked the friars to come and scatter ashes on his head.

And while the brothers were gathered around him in intense and moving prayer, he went to sleep in the Lord, and his soul, freed from his body, was taken into the immense love of God.

28

It was 3 October 1226 and Francis was not yet forty-five years old.

RUFFINELLI

The last salute of all the creatures

Just at the moment of the poor man's death, the sister skylarks, which loved the light and were so afraid of the dark, even though the night was falling, flew in a great flock in wide circles for a long time over the little church of St Mary of the Angels.

The birds gave forth a joyous song, as if to pay tribute, honour, and glory to the saint who so many times had invited them to praise God and who had called them 'sisters'.

At the first light of dawn, since the news of Francis' death spread quickly, residents of Assisi came to venerate the saint's body in the place of St Mary called Portiuncula.

There were men, women, and above all children. The children carried in their hands branches of trees as did the children when Jesus entered the city of Jerusalem.

And truly on that holy night blessed Francis, accompanied by the song of all the creatures, entered into the Jerusalem of the heavens to sing with the angels the praises of the most high.

So closed the earthly life of this man, merciful, and always ready to pardon and show compassion. The man who more than any other, resembled in his life that of Christ and who, more than any other, loved all creatures of the universe, great and small, living and not living.

The man who above all loved God tenderly, Father and Creator of Brother Sun and of Sister Moon, and of the stars, and of Mother Earth, and of all creatures which it sustains.